Keeping Count

M. Travis Lane

Guelph, Ontario

Published with the generous assistance of Scott and April Snider.

Edited by Shane Neilson
Cover and book design by Jeremy Luke Hill
Proofreading by Carol Dilworth
Set in Athelas
Printed on Mohawk Via Felt
Printed and bound by Arkay Design & Print

LIBRARY AND ARCHIVES CANADA CATALOGUING IN PUBLICATION

Title: Keeping count / M. Travis Lane.
Names: Lane, M. Travis (Millicent Travis), 1934- author.
Description: Poems.
Identifiers: Canadiana (print) 20200221213 | Canadiana (ebook) 20200221221
| ISBN 9781774220054 (softcover) | ISBN 9781774220061 (PDF)
| ISBN 9781774220078 (HTML)
Classification: LCC PS8573.A55 K44 2020 | DDC C811/.54—dc23

Gordon Hill Press respectfully acknowledges the ancestral homelands of the Attawandaron, Anishinaabe, Haudenosaunee, and Metis Peoples, and recognizes that we are situated on Treaty 3 territory, the traditional territory of Mississaugas of the Credit First Nation.

Gordon Hill Press also recognizes and supports the diverse persons who make up its community, regardless of race, age, culture, ability, ethnicity, nationality, gender identity and expression, sexual orientation, marital status, religious affiliation, and socioeconomic status.

Gordon Hill Press
130 Dublin Street North
Guelph, Ontario, Canada
N1H 4N4
www.gordonhillpress.com

with gratitude for friends, editors, family – above all, for readers

TABLE OF CONTENTS

THE YOUNG BOBCAT

A young bobcat
leaned on the door of the old-age home,
a "native woodnote" not yet wild.
Don't let it in.

Look at the yard.
The trees are cut.
The grass is not original.
There might be ants,
domestic, small.

Now that the world's so simplified
we have to invent
the wilderness we do not have.

And yet the shadows of our dreams
from an alternative universe,
(to which we do not want to go)
affirm the limitations of our sight.

Perhaps we should take a photograph.

OUTSIDE

THE RIVER IS CLOTTED WITH SCUTTLED ICE

The river is clotted with scuttled ice,
the ponds still jeweled.
Geese overhead are returning –
their long mist-piercing necks, their cries!

Mallards, the cock pearl-emerald,
the hen-brown grass,
float on the melted shallows of a stream
their landscape floating riverward.

In the roadside bush the remnants
of past snow cling like wet tissues;
the verge is bald, clay-streaked
and steaming. In the ditch
runnels of black water
tinged with green.

Follow the wet unfoldings of the day:
the flooded meadows, the tidal marsh,
red clay, salt-jagged. And by the shore,
foam pelting the water with tiny strafe.
Stand on the sea edge of the wharf.
A seal's head bobbing like a toy peers up at us.
Day pounds. The salt wind stings.

MURMURATION

A loose concentric of tiny birds
settles into a demi-lune
veiling a naked tree.

In silhouette
they seem the ghosts of blackened leaves,
small consonants the wind obscures.

Then lifting off, regathering,
they billow against the whitening sky,

as if a music had shut up,
a poem eased.
They vanished into their vanishing.

LAMÈQUE

Whittled by wind into barrenness:
the motel, the café,
the salt-rimed lot
where we could have parked.

At the jetty edge
the water seemed
almost subdued,
the beach weeds white.

Cold, brilliant, tidy–
we could have walked but didn't–
(sand in the air, leg scouring)–

A lighthouse rang
for weather we hadn't
expected yet,

the fishing boats
already in harbour.

LATE FALL

The long boughs of the dying elms
are draining the sky of its evening glow;
below them unclad windows:
        yellow-gold parentheses.

*

The highway glimmers;
the concrete bridge
sands with snow.
        Black water jets under it.

*

The wind has swung the store signs round about,
a frieze of hail on the power lines.
        An airplane, over-nighting, pricks the sky.

*

Morning's leavening sky
strings broken mists
elsewhere to decipher a valley.
        A fox returns to its wind-shagged den.

THE SATELLITE

Lonely, perhaps, impertinent, the "star"
that sometimes in the morning stares
as if it were significant
but not, like stars, reliable –

like some huge, astral streetlight shines
as if it needed to be seen –

its eastern pose a clown's pretense,
as steady as it seems at dawn,
a solid astral diamond,
tomorrow it may not be there

but will have gone
to stare, still blind, still ignorant,
at someone else's night.

BOW RIVER

The river runs white, or nearly so,
reflecting the disposals of the sky,
though sometimes with a tinge of green,
blue-green, pea soup, or celadon,
as if the dwarfed trees at its edge
discoloured their reflections on its flow.

A scarf of silk, a highway for white beasts,
it's dangerous;
what crosses it might founder.
It pulls the scree from the frost-cracked hills,
chafing the rust-stained glaciers,
it seems a monstrous waterfall
lain flat as if for ironing.
A cold cloth, calmly violent,
it scours the fence-bound highway with its nap.

THE NORTH IS RECEDING

The north is receding. A tropic wind
preceding a dead tropic eye
has been thrashing the aspen, the browning pines.

But now the wind's pulled in its claws,
basks on our hot garden, pulls
the humid foreign air
across us, and the heat

prickles our skin: a tropic rash
that leaves no scars
except below our sleep-starved eyes.

All night the highway mutters; sirens scream;
lights from the street flash over us
a muted blare –
we must have slept.

Perhaps we dreamed
of the saline rust of oceans or
the deserts that we humans make:
no trees, no grass, no water, but
as beautiful as this night's moon –

which has no air.

MARCH WIND

Wind opens the day, an enormous door.
The snowy hollows come undone;
small roofless caves
like sinkholes in eternity,
they glitter with space.

The light shrieks out
from the leafless trees
and splinters my thoughts.
Like last year's leaves
they scatter, flotsam on the zest
of spring's unmindful violence.

QUIET

Far down the river at the Point
someone has lit a cigarette.
Above us the orange heavens sprawl
brilliant, indifferent, ignorant.
The river sloshes gently. The whippoorwill's
monotonous request, ecstatic frogs,
cicadas buzz and bury themselves
in palmetto breeze
that fans the river's mirror which reflects
the opal sky. The shuffling step
of some small mammal might disrupt
the evening's peace, but doesn't.
Quiet enough.

GHOST TOWN

Below a blue, overhanging peak
a drift of miner's houses:
news-papered walls, tin roofs.

The lanky moon keeps swaggering through
the small details of death and birth.
The town, a pillow of dry leaves,
disintegrates.

THE PATH TO NOWHERE

The tree that held the world up lost its grasp.
The stars that sifted through its twigs, no longer tuned,
jangle and fade.

One song, perhaps, reknits it, tangle or nest,
like the string hand games that children play,
a lover's knot redone, redoing,
yes –

but pull a thread:
music turns into a parking lot–
alder and swamp and the heavy moss
dissolving under the streetlight's drench,
becoming the path to nowhere which

we must not take.

A WHOLE LIFETIME

(J. H. Latude, prisoner 1725-1805)

Small clouds like scuffed leaves cross the sky.
A freckled sun blotches the donjon at Vincennes,
its cold, choleric forehead, with gold qualms.
A guard's child's scarlet tricycle
sprawls on the paving – a horse half-curbed,
a courier's.

Blockaded from this airy fuss, the prisoner,
hunched over his hearthstones, scraped
a shinny route for rags: epistles
of years in blood from his deaf cell
to prisoners less imprisoned in the yard.

"I live" is all the letters said.

INSIDE

DO YOU REMEMBER?

Do you remember the alder woods
where we used to camp?
Overgrown now, with aspen, larch,
and hackmatack.

I slept there once in a hammock,
a roofed tarpaulin
whose net sides let in saline air.
Small creatures thumping over me,
their tiny feet
dinted its roof.

Dew in the morning: we lit a fire.
Remember tea in plastic mugs,
the wetness of green raspberries?

Remember those autumns when blueberry hills
were patch-worked magenta, crimson, orange,

and those grey sand shores where swirling birds
opened and closed the evening skies?

I remember trying to photograph
what was mostly air. I remember, too,

the long drive home, together, and
fields of broken cornstalks
turning brown.

COUNTING NEIGHBOURS

Three in the morning they started up,
shrill, operatic. There must be more than one,
such theatre!
I've only seen them twice, both times
as solitary trundlers, haunches high, head down,
at dusk, along the back fence, going home
next door below their shed, or back from mine.

Also the silent snuffler, peacock-tailed,
a fountain of black/white I've seen at dawn;
I find its grub holes in my lawn (saves the expense
of pesticide.) The cats don't mind.
With coons or skunks they keep a truce.

With squirrels, however, it's different:
the small red one who runs along the fence,
almost always alone,
the grey squirrels who remade their nest
that fell down from in the windstorm, and,
the chipmunks, the conciergerie
who sit on my front doorstep as if I
were less important than a leaf,

and chickadees, sparrows, and always crows
(those colonies that, winter-times,
hang in loose crowds like swarming bees),
pigeons of course, and a hummingbird
I never see 'til summer, late, robins
in fair quantity, finches, grosbeaks, once
even, briefly, a sparrow-hawk.

Out front the students wander past.
Should I count them?
Should I count the gnats? the spiders? bees?
And you, if you come to visit me,
may I count you?

YOU ARE THE PAUSE

(*variations on Rilke's* Book of Hours, *no. 20*)

You are the pause between two words,
the words not said, not thought of yet,

a breath not breathed.

You slide upon the freedom of "not yet,"
not "done," not "sure to come."

You are the absolute of now,
which, time uncovering, slips
into the stream of nothingness.

You are the pause between two words,
not said, not even thought of yet.

LIVE IN HD

The smell of rancid butter, slightly scorched,
drenches the crowded atrium.

Outside snow falls on the parking lot,
a trifle dreary, but mystical
in the softened neon of afternoon.

The mall is crowded, sleazy,
warm. A prototype for Paradise?
Almost. Friendly, comfortable.

But that semi-forest across the street
seems nearer to a paradise
I could imagine, beautiful –

but I can't stroll
among those winter-blistered trees,
the candled tufts of withered weeds
skimming the thin-iced pond.

Here I can wait for the opera,
warm, friendly, safe –

the video games still audible,
and the smell of rancid butter, slightly scorched.

FOR RUTH

Days cluster, days clutter – they open, shut,
heap on the bed like feather quilts.
I can nest in them – pulling the good cloth
over me, letting the old cat lick my thighs –

which is all I have left. Though sometimes, nights,
I feel beside me my husband's weight,
as if his ear plug radio
had lulled him to sleep with its baseball games
(so like the old cat's rasping purr
I had grown fond of, or used to).

What day is it now? I have lost track.
My notebooks by the bed have grown
stale, dusty. (I know it's night.)
But that's OK.
It's not right now that I need to know.
Someone will tell me
what I can't be bothered remembering –

though "remember" is what I do.

"IN YOUR SILLY MOOD"

(for Allen Ginsberg)

A focused irritation like a match
that burns the cupping fingers:
a forced imagination stalls.
Fuel? Batteries? A CD choir
honeys the dry, dust-scented air.
It's no big deal.
Wind fingers the tarnished juniper.
I could lean here on this music like a bed
and watch the sun drift slowly past
like a scorched tide. And now a flute,
a bird in a different planet's woods.

Not mine, not mine – the music tires
and my head hurts. A wintered soul?
What is the best use of today
I ought to ask, and don't.
Sleep? Coffee? The perpetual chores?
The numb reiterations of a book?

MAY ROCKS

Spring. The May rocks butt and push,
the soft lawn's jagged with dragon's teeth.
New stones rise up, while last year's stones
sink under moss
as if the mud were pulling back
what it so strongly had put forth,
the mud inconstant, fidgety.

The house, too, teeters on its slab,
perched as it is on deciduous rock.
The water that melts down our hill
erodes the city underground,
silts up the gravel river-plain.
The planet itself is no sure thing,
though, mornings, I'd want to bet on it.

MEDUXNEKEAG

Grey felted leaves like dry mouse skins
covered the path. The leafless trees
seemed tarnished by the afternoon
that flickered among them like a bird
which, never precisely where we looked,
was not quite out of sight.

Black posts defined the forest trail
which wandered, uneven, irresolute –
we thought we heard water, or maybe wind –
the steady noise of shuffling, that was us,
but mostly silence. The market posts
kept turning into spindly trees
too thin to support us. A silty dust
slid under our feet as we clung to rocks.

Without you I couldn't have managed it.
You pulled me over massive stones
past a deep bear cave, fragrant,
but still untenanted.

Beyond us a tangle of bush and briar,
the hilltop blocked by a storm-felled pine,
a giant, forest guardian, still green,
the bleeding root mass twice my height –
(think of the white pine navies we have cut,
the lumbered cedars of Lebanon)
a tree for Wotan, not for us.
It blocked our path.

We turned around.
Picking our way through underbrush,
through spikes of adolescent spruce,
down hill, down hill –

and found ourselves at the forest's foot,
the river, flat, unhurried, where
small iridescent minnows swam
in shallows of gold sand.

TOO QUIET

It gets *too* quiet
mid-afternoon, midwinter:
no cars, no bus, no students,
and no wind.

The furnace has stopped its mumbling.
The floor seems cold and high
as if a sleep
thumbed out its ride.

I hear
the vaporizer steaming,
the kitchen clock,
and, yes, a car has driven by –

so I've not jelled quite solid yet,
(although the walls
seem curving inward, nothing straight,
and all the pictures lean out toward the dusk).

It seems that only yesterday
I heard the diesel's sombre cry.
Sometimes the clock cathedral rang
each hour, or so I thought it did.
And then of course the evening winds
shaking the grey elm ridgepoles of bleak night.

What elms? What trains?
My ghosts are broad awake
and seem to follow after me
as if they wanted to be fed – small, feeble,
dusty, shadow-folk.

Me too. I need a wakening.
A dawn midday, a sort of door.
A mind let rest
finds nothingness. Or sleep.

MY OLD PAL VENUS

Oh yes, my old pal Venus –
there she is – or ought to be.
One moment and that brilliant light
will have sunk below the hospital
that rims the hilltop of our street.
(The lesser lights, that seem to spire
away from her, subsided, too.)

I went outdoors to search
pin prickles in a flannel sky –
no waiting here for the Perseids,
our heavens scummed by street-lamps,
cars – as if to keep us local, fixed.

Now, as I drag the trash can out,
not even the North Star still beams through.
The moon, a little cockeyed, glints.
I'm grateful for the company,
such as it is.

MARKET

A market almost without food:
some green bananas, biscuits in bright tins,
baskets of strident, knitted gloves, a bin
of squeaky toys for dogs,

dozens of hand-planed cutting boards,
little Swiss knives, a stall
of long pashminas price-reduced,

and, iced, in a corner, a tub of trout
pearly with iridescent slime,
blind-eyed, gutted, and

nearby, a shelf of home-made vinegars,
imported patés, lace underpants,
and bottle-top boards, for collectors of.
There were no eggs.

Outside the market building a small man
sat shivering on a folding chair
with his paper cup.

"Support your local business"
said the sign outside the market door.
I bought a trout.

THE CROSSING

The S. S. *General Buckner* smelled
like stale dish rags. Wind
blew from the galley toward the chairs
where we sat outside.
Inside was worse.

There was nothing to see:
the flat Pacific, mumbling, grey.
The nights were cloudy with no stars.
Three weeks in a sort of mindless world
while the troopship caterpillar-crawled
across the drabness of the sea.

There was nothing to do. "Events"
for grownups. I babysat. Or read in my berth.
The films were duds,
insipid or shoddy.
You could see the shadows of the bars
of the tiger's cage against the palms:
"There will be white bait," said the heroine,
tying herself.
Queasy, I ate saltines, green grapes.

No birds, no fish, but once,
not far from the ship, a bobbing globe,
black – not a whale as we had hoped –
a mine left over from the war,
thrown out like picnic litter, we supposed.
No one seemed to be bothered by it.

I read Okinawan history
from the army brochure. Savage it seemed.
Like the books I got from the library,
it didn't seem real.

One family had books they had brought on board.
I read, while I watched their children sleep,
a book of large grey photographs:
Dachau, Auschwitz.

And then one dawn:
a silk sea lucent with jelly moons,
pine islets inked by Hokusai –
and Fuji, white-fanned, in the west –
the beauty of an antique scroll,
almost familiar, improbable.

"But that's real," I thought.
"Like the other things: the mine,
and the prison camps."

HOW CAN WE SEE WHAT WE'RE LOOKING AT?

How can we see what we're looking at
if someone's not told us first?
Doesn't a mother tell her child
meanings, at least, before the words?

Remember that kidnapped Beothuk,
returning from his London trip,
only reported what fitted in
the stories he knew how to say.

Not relevant the other stuff
his condescending captors showed.
What could he *see*? Or rather, *what could he say*?

Consider that family photograph:
the happy kids
are squinting their eyes against the sun,
but one, in the shade, has looked away.

I couldn't read that as "the suicide."
But someone said. She saw it in the gesture,
in the shade. But was it there in the photograph?

She knew the family narrative.

THE SEA SWIMS INTO MY ROOM AT NIGHT

The sea swims into my room at night.
They say it is the moonlight, but the floor
trembles; the wind can alter it;
the glittering waters bathe my feet
with their cold salt.

The windows are a field of ice
that cracks and splinters as the house
shudders against its mooring. Mist
from starlight coats my hands. The polar dusk
blossoms, releases my iron dreams
which bob up and away from me
like bubbles of black air. Light
waits below water, invisible.

WE RELIED ON THE MOON

We relied on the moon
or the moon's reflection.
It was somewhere else
we could not reach:
a mirror, sad, and feminine,
a sort of garden ornament.

That moon is lost.
Nature, wild, and on its own,
retains a silvery loveliness.
We still feel kindly when the moon
lets down her long white strokes on us
and we can sleep.

Easily then. Less easy now.

THE SHOUT

A storm last night. The surly day
still wrings its sullen handkerchief.
There may have been some warning,
not enough.

Angry at loss a youngster shouts
as if against the deafness of the sea.
No one seems to be listening.

His language falls in splinters.
"Listen!" he cries, but all he hears
is water, water, water,
thudding against the beach.

WHAT ON EARTH WERE WE LOOKING FOR?

A tulip cups the yellow light,
a hand torch in the quickening dusk.
Shadows have filled the drainage ditch.
The narrow path furs over.
It won't be tonight we make it to
the fabled Gate of Happiness.

What would there be but an effigy
grinning serenely, or dancing like a star
whose brilliance bears no messages?
Here in the backyard of the soul
sadness is real, and pain.

The tulip's glow
shows only the path, although
its fragrance all night comforts us,
a kind of companion, after all.
Happiness, like cotton candy, cloys.
What on earth were we looking for?

IMAGINING OUR ORIGINS

The melodies splash on our shores,
disintegrate, and under us
the sand, dissolving, moves our feet.
We, too, seem distanter each day –
and yet imagine that each sound
runs backward toward the edge of light –
as if, were we only fast enough,
we could be always where that shout
proclaimed existence first, or as if song
were something we could navigate,
in all this widening ocean, ride.

NIGHT IS THE GRAND CATHEDRAL

Night is the grand cathedral but
we do not go to worship there.
When waiting on a dying child
among machines and magazines,
or watching under a poor-laid thatch,
we can not think we celebrate,
yet watching is a sacrament.

Night's glittering blanket covers us,
conceals, as if we need not know,
under the stars, our uselessness.
Perhaps it's darkness lets us know
we are not scraps or litter. In the night,
asleep, returning to the lap
of our originating pulse,
we are priest, bread –
and sacrifice.

MOTHER OF ALL

Mother of all, with your night blue cloak
beneath which creep
your multi-coloured children in their rags
of pain, starvation, poverty,
be for us all a shelter, lantern, ship.

The moths fly toward your halo,
char and burn: you are not kind.
And is your night sky over us
a cave in which we carve ideas,
each life a shard, a tessera
in the anointed frescoes of your vault?

We crave, we doubt:
the shadows fall.

You can not change; our suffering is yours,
as are our sicknesses – victims of ourselves
and change, the lead weight of life's gravity.
Our numbers pulse and flutter on your screen;
our protozoan efforts flash and flail.
All you can do is gather them:
a dewdrop in the center of your hand.

THE ROCKING CHAIR IN THE RECOVERY ROOM

Beauty, compassion, kindliness
reach out to us as though they were one creature,
as in our minds they are;
a self-engendered holiness
of love we think so integral to nature
we can't imagine war –
a child deliberately hacked,
raped, tortured – facts
harder than myths to hold in mind.

In the rocking chair in the recovering room
she lulls her child with his bandaged hand,
singing what God, we think, must sing:
the seed song of the universe –
as if all troubles must come home
and leave us in the soft arms of a nurse,
recovering, a wounded child possessed
by the one gift God can not have
(for God, as God, can only love).

For now, the baby sleeps upon her breast,
human, imperfect, injured, and unkind.

WE MUST GIVE THANKS

Dawn, and the pallid baby turns its eyes,
an instinct of commitment that
even when dying we sometimes have,
if sometimes, life forgive me, I forget.

Like tightrope walkers on a line
we hope is there, or like
disciples on thin water over stones
we hope lie underneath the waves –
we might not drown.

His line did snap. As ours will too.
And yet his ghost
walks with us, suffers, dies again,
a human god.
We are ashamed of our fearfulness.

We must give thanks for courage
when it comes. We must
pick up our beds, our sickly child,

and cross what might be water
over stones.

SCAR

A foolish rain sluices the street,
erases it.

A sullen fist of shadows slides
into the gutter, anonymous.

Spite shatters the harmless afternoon.
Like a split in film,
it needs to be patched.

The scar is trivial,
permanent.

NO DICE

God doesn't "play dice,"
so Einstein said.
A Calvinist assuredness.

Like that boxed cat
whose fate already is.
(Our knowing's not significant.)

But some things slip.
No donkey starves
between two bales.

The arrow and the tortoise
reach their goals.
As for the cat –

you should let it out.

VELASQUEZ'S INFANTA

The Infanta, like a doll with her not-yet-lived-in face,
centres our attention. Next to her
the graceful maid, the watchful dog.
Beside them a discarded toy:
the dwarf, no longer cute, tear-shorn.

Beyond the doll in shadow
the adults hover by a door
that opens to a world the child's not known,
as if the theme
of an unripened innocence
erases their complicities.

The formal sun
blazes on her china face,
caresses her stiff petticoats.
Even the dog knows something she can't know.

This painting's like a finger in a book
that stops our reading to reflect:
of all the people figured here,
she, only, has no voice.

SARCEN

Not quite like a pastured elephant
whose devious independence yet allows
greed, curiosity, the shout
of a familiar, turn
its boulder body toward the fence,
this thing has ceased to answer us.

Though mind had moved it once
and set it where its blindness stares
toward the accumulating nights,
its gestures grown illegible –
yet here, among the crow-browse, seems at home.
We, in its field, are alien.

ERASURES

As if we were lice,
the ocean combs us out –
a sort of scummy litter on its fringe.

Now Vulcan's plated armour shifts
beneath the weight of scarlet caves,
those hot, disputing labyrinths
indifferent to us.

Weren't we all milky babes at first?
The cruel will die no sooner than the rest.
The swamping sea floods over us,
erasures on the blackboard of the beach.

STICK

"Bend like water; like water bite."
Advice. But what am I?
A stick tossed on the current. I
can't bend, can't bite, can't
mark my way.

I've had my green leaves and my bloom.
Now dry, I sense the pull
of oceans I can't navigate,
nor can I choose one threaded flow
among the rocks, muds, effluent,

but like a stick a child has thrown
into a river, I bob and turn –
thrown, and thrown away.

BACK AT DOVER

(for Matthew Arnold)

Like you
I heard
the roar and fumble of approach,
withdrawing sighs,
the surly grate
of stone on stone
becoming sand,

the armour tread of history
which polishes
its disappointing anecdotes
and shakes us loose,
unsteady,
where we stand.

The sea
recovers its steel surfaces.
mirrors
that the moon sweeps clear.

Against continual motion we
hang upon each other's lives
as if they were strong ropes thrown out –
to save us,
but –
how can they be?
We being water,
harbourless,
and subject to continual change.

HOMESICK FOR WHAT?

Homesick for what?
The old dog's dead;
the meadow's turned into a trailer park.
Those dark wire-tufted blackberries
he nibbled on, and the heavy grass
where he'd settle down,
waiting for us to be ready to go
(as if road pebbles hurt his paws)
is asphalt: convenience, snacks, and toys.

Better a map that is out of date
than these new ones which show
only the places we've never been,
blotting the ones we know!

Onward and upward!
Up is hard –
like an old fashioned ski-tow –
I hold on;
the rope skids through my mittens.

I'm still here;
it hurts a little less each time
to grab, to clutch, and then let go.

I've gained an inch.
Mark that in snow.

DIARY

The fields, the river, the office blocks
are salmon pink.
The ink etched scrawl of naked trees
cross over them
as if a child had scribbled on a book.

Close to my window the juniper
hangs shriveled hands,
as if they could not lift, extend
towards light as they ought to do.

The glassy sunset's brilliance, like a match
flares, and, as if the clouds were smoke,
extinguishes: an urban grey
punctured by city lights.

Nothing will last,
and most things don't repeat,
except in somewhat variant form.
We grow to recognise the dark
as if it, diary, turned a page –

always worth reading –

THE COMFORT THAT WE KNEW

Without intention, joy, or grief,
we crumble like a faded leaf:
to dust to rock to starry plain –
a different life starts up again –

not mine, not yours, but new
and, like our own, is transient.
And love   and love?
is still our home.

Be patient.

WATCHING TV WITH DAVY

Cat Davy and I were watching TV,
hoping they'd show us something else
on Baffin, not just the cold, grey sea
and empty shores, silent,
except for the narrator.

We watched the coloured lichen, moss
growing on stones against which moved
(and we sat up):
two tiny beasts,
orange, avid, furred!

As if in a blasted universe
these still-encrypted moths
burrowed – mundane
and unimportant,
just like us
embedded in the sofa.

The soul does have its wakenings,
its caterpillar springs.

THE STARS ARE SURER THAN WE ARE

The stars are surer than we are, though they throw fits
from time to time (not in our seasons but in theirs).
What in the sky are we sure about?
We've grown so long accustomed to the same
progression of the planets, but from us,
don't we want somehow difference?
Perhaps we do.

But not the difference we get.
        (So I lost you.)

A STAR EXPLODED THE OTHER DAY

A star exploded the other day.
I saw it on the news.

> (So fragile is our universe: the dew
> that diamonds the spider's net
> an option of our galaxy.)

Is it enough to be beautiful?

You, walking barefoot on the grass,
a foray into the web of time –

> *(I love you of course.)*

Does that matter much?

WAY OUT

THE FALL OF LIGHT

The fall of light, the shadows that,
as day progresses, twist and change,
faint, feline, elusive –

is this enough?

(Two waxwings in the backyard crab,
glitter of phone lines, rainbow-iced) –

"Take it easy," I'm told.
Easy it is:
the breath
that I have to stop to catch –

and the fall of light
is beautiful.

WALKING MORE SLOWLY

When we walked at first
beside each other I had to run,
almost, a little, to keep up with you
(your long legs striding).
You led the way
through the bush-grown paths.
Our Dolly dog ran back and forth
between us, as you forged ahead.

Later I walked ahead of you, turned round,
with Pip dog I walked back to you,
our thirty steps to your fifteen.
I remember your gentle shuffling,
determined to keep on.

But that was then.
I walk more slowly on my own.

THE SERGEANT MAJOR

Death, like a sergeant major, shouts
at our staggering queue.
Oh yes, dear friend,
you hear him squall and yet resist
as strongly as a weak body can.
The rest of us
(LEFT RIGHT LEFT RIGHT)
just carry on.
Where is that fellow taking us?

Your cats, who do not read the weather on the news,
behave like cats, a good idea, but
will this be when the Gulf Stream drops,
enough? YOU won't be here.
Your coming battle is too soon;
you wage it tiny bit by bit.
I hear you laugh, between the shots,
the pills for pain.

What can the good Lord make of you
but snatch you up?
We, busy, healthy, have no time –
and time, in its molasses trickling,
has no space.
When, when I come to visit you,
should I say good-bye?

TRUDGE

(*Isaiah 52:7*)

To speak without embarrassment of serious things
requires an adult heart, for which
the oldness of new things does not require disguise,
for which the self with all its shades
(those fads, those envies – all that stuff)
is simply what we carry, like our feet:
no longer beautiful these days, not "bearers
of good news," but can, along the mountain tops,
still trudge.

OUTSIDE FOR AN HOUR

(*Windsor Court*)

It must be a bus that every night
casts its weak flare across the wall.
I can't read clock time in the dark
but press my finger to the bell:
someone will come.

Helped up, sponged off, and tucked back in –
how long will it be to breakfast time?

*

Four to a table. One
can't talk. One
won't. Dear Fraser will.
(He has nothing to say.)
No music, no news,
wheeled back to my cell.

*

Rain or the air conditioner
pounds in a gentle monotone.
Down hall four large exotic fish
drift sucking and nibbling their tank's glass sides.

Outside the bedroom window a sky shred
has twisted like the handle of a purse.

Will you come today?

The flowers have died on the window sill.

*

I sit in my wheelchair. An hour outside,
motion in a universe of want.
The "guests" lined up on the patio
don't speak. They smile back when I smile at them,
then let their faces fall apart
into the rags of abandoned age
for which they seem to apologise.

I've been reading indoors. Outside
no book, an almost bugless lawn,
the sidewalk to the patio, and an abandoned garden
trough
("something to do" –
a geriatrician's fantasy.)

My wheelchair's stuck in the molting lawn;
there are no birds, no flies.

Count ants:
the little brown ants that course
their single paving block as if it were a mystery.
Are there four or five?
A large black ant heads straight up hill
as if across a continent,
a sort of concrete Darien.

The minders have set out plastic rings
to throw in a box.
“Show what you’re made of!”
they shout at their limp clientele.

I ring my help bell, am brought in.

THE INJURED MOUSE IN THE PARKING LOT

1. Recluse

"Am I famous?" he asked.
The neighborhood
don't mind. He puts his garbage out
in time, is quiet. When we come
to visit, to replenish his small hoard
of Cup-of-Soup, V-8, and books,
he finds our children easier than us.
Perhaps in another life, he says,
things would improve.

2. The High School Chorus Entertains

The audience were "ill." We sang
"You are my sunshine" and "Irene."
"How nice of us," the staff said, but –

one of the patients hated me.

3. Afternoon at the Nursing Home

My old friend smiled. "10, 7, 12,"
is what she said. She almost danced
in her wheelchair, patting the floor
with her slippered feet.
I should have answered in numbers but
I didn't. I held out my hand.
(Her hands were tied.)
"64, 12, 92," she said,
gaily, and paddled away.

4. She Had To

She had to drive him to emergency.
She had seen the devil in his cheek
and had tried to cut it out.

"Is your husband afraid of *you*?" she asked.

5. The Injured Mouse in the Parking Lot

I saw it
running in a tight circle, nose to tail.
Dying, I thought.

Its passionate running –

END NOTE: DEEP LISTENING

I first heard of Janet Thom Hammock's Deep Listening Institute when she read from her essays on "deep listening" at Fredericton's "Odd Sundays" poetry readings.

I think I have always gone in for "deep listening" but especially now as my hearing decreases. Had I as a child ever heard silence? So many of my memories of childhood seem connected with sounds. Water and weather of course. The aches and creaks of a house – and the groans, ticks, and murmurs of the machines within it. The thumps and scurrying of cats, the roof thuds of squirrels, and, scraping about in the walls, my unpaying tenants who leave their tiny turds along the top of the basement bookcase.

Then there's the street with its cars, the bus, the buzzing street lights, its chatty or (late night) drunken students – and the highway, not all that close, but constantly in roar. No matter how late at night it is, I can hear the highway. And all those beasts: the hunting owl, the courting raccoons – someone downtown has bought fireworks – and there is the ambulance once again!

If I go out to the forest, aren't the trees noisy? Cracking or whining or rattling their branches. And brooks do babble! Even the pond taps gently at its spongy rim.

I no longer hear bats, some birds. Mumbling, whispering poets have merged for me into the sounds of water on stone or wind on trees.

I remember, in Costa Rica, lying still in a slightly creaking hammock under more stars than I had ever imagined, with the waves patting the seacoast, and distant thunder lighting, occasionally, the horizon's rim. The candle on the table next to me uttered a tiny, somewhat prickling, sigh.

PUBLICATION HISTORY

Some of these poems have appeared in *EVENT Magazine, The Fiddlehead, GUEST, Numero Cinq*, *Riddle Fence,* and *The Walrus.*

ABOUT THE AUTHOR

One of Canada's most distinguished writers, M. Travis Lane lives in Fredericton, New Brunswick. She received her B.A. (Junior PBK) from Vassar College, and her M.A. and PhD. from Cornell University. She and her husband Lauriat Lane came to New Brunswick in 1960. Travis taught briefly at Cornell and at the University of New Brunswick and is a Honorary Research Associate with the English Department at U.N.B. She is a member of the Voice of Women for Peace and a Raging Granny, a member of the Writer's Federation of New Brunswick and a Lifetime member of the League of Canadian Poets.

Lane has published eighteen books of poetry and two of prose. She has received numerous awards for her writing, including the Pat Lowther Memorial Award, the Alden Nowlan Award for Excellence in Literary Arts, and the Lieutenant Governor's Award for High Achievement in Literary Arts. She was also shortlisted for the Governor General's Award for Poetry in 2015.